Jon Scieszka's TRUCKTOWN

It Is Hot!

Pete

Dan

Adapted by Alison Hawes

Illustrated by DESIGN garage

"I can see Pete," said Dan.

Pete is hot.

"I can see the sun," said Dan.

The sun is hot.

"I can see a fan," said Dan.

The fan is **not** hot.

"I can not see Pete!" said Dan.